P9-DOC-644

The Virginia Colony

Tamara L. Britton

ABDO Publishing Company

Published by ABDO Publishing Company, 4940 Viking Drive, Edina, Minnesota 55435.

Printed in the United States.

Cover Photo Credit: North Wind Picture Archives
Interior Photo Credits: North Wind Picture Archives (pages 7, 9, 11, 13, 15, 17, 18, 20, 27, 29), Corbis (pages 19, 21, 23, 25)

Contributing Editors: Kate A. Furlong and Christine Fournier
Book Design and Graphics: Neil Klinepier, Bob Italia

Library of Congress Cataloging-in-Publication Data

Britton, Tamara L., 1963-
The Virginia Colony / Tamara L. Britton.
p. cm. -- (The colonies)
Includes index.
ISBN 1-57765-579-6
1. Virginia--History--Colonial period, ca. 1600-1775--Juvenile literature. [1. Virginia--History--Colonial period, ca. 1600-1775.] I. Title. II. Series.

F229 .B848 2001
975.5'02--dc21

2001018868

Contents

Virginia

Native Americans first settled present-day Virginia. The most powerful tribe was the Powhatan (poh-haw-tin). It had nearly 9,000 members.

Europeans explored present-day Virginia in the 1500s. In 1607, the Virginia Company began a colony there. It was England's first permanent colony in North America.

The colonists built a settlement called Jamestown. The first years at Jamestown were difficult. But soon colonists had built houses and successful tobacco farms.

Soon, French colonists and Virginians began arguing over land. This led to a war. Then England began taxing many goods the colonists needed.

The colonists thought the new taxes were unfair. So all the colonies joined together. They went to war with England. The colonists won the war. Then they created the United States of America. Virginia became the tenth state of the new nation.

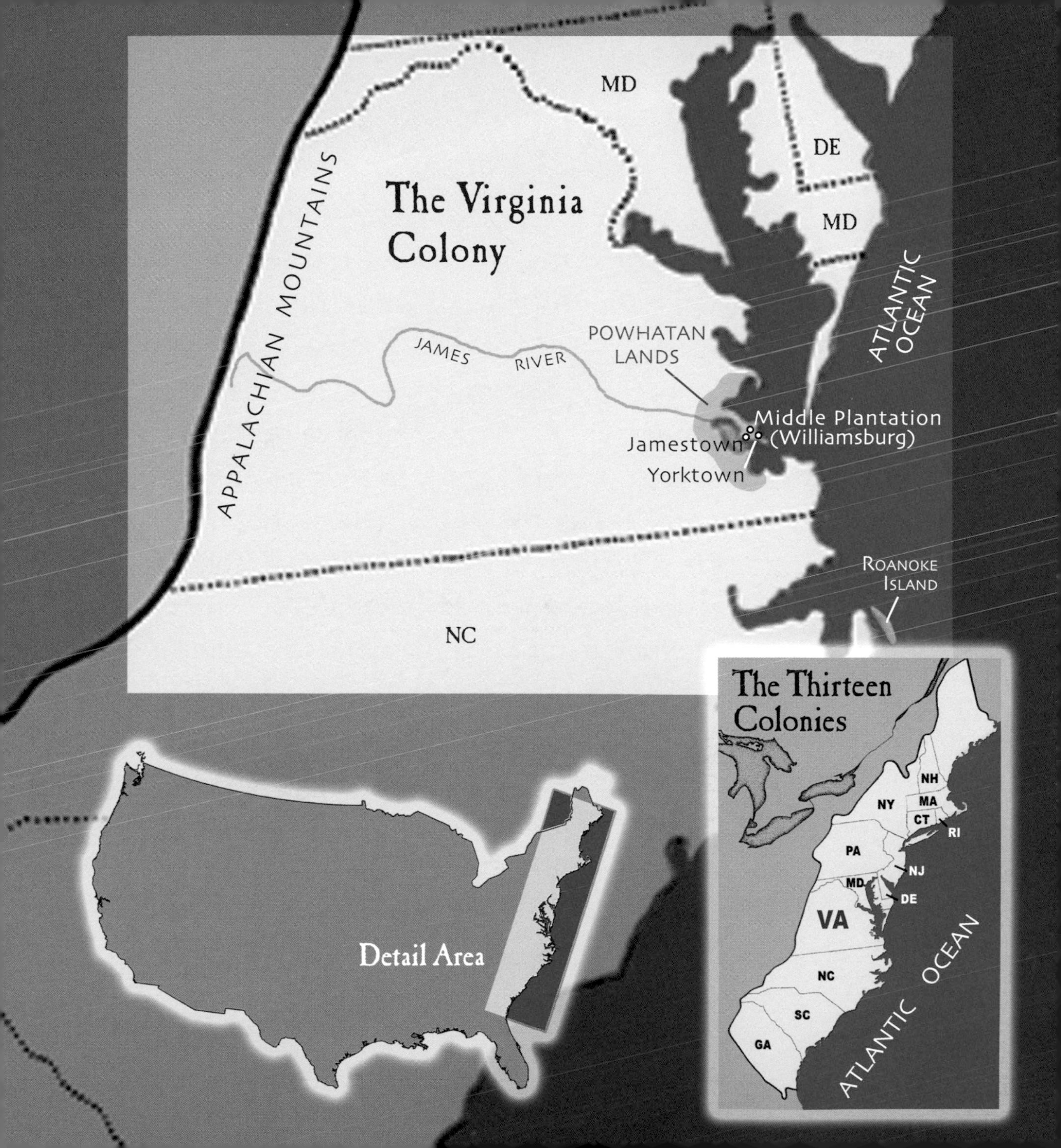

The Virginia Colony

MD
DE
MD
APPALACHIAN MOUNTAINS
ATLANTIC OCEAN
POWHATAN LANDS
JAMES RIVER
Middle Plantation (Williamsburg)
Jamestown
Yorktown
ROANOKE ISLAND
NC

The Thirteen Colonies

NH
MA
NY
CT
RI
PA
NJ
MD
DE
VA
NC
SC
GA
ATLANTIC OCEAN

Detail Area

Early Days

Virginia is on the Atlantic Coast. The Appalachian (ap-uh-LAY-shun) Mountains run through western Virginia. Central Virginia is a **plateau**. Eastern Virginia is a low, coastal plain. Many rivers run from the mountains down to the Atlantic Ocean. Virginia has a mild climate.

Virginia's first settlers were Native Americans. They spoke Algonquian (al-GON-kwee-an), Iroquois (EAR-oh-kwoy), and Sioux (SOO) languages. Virginia's most powerful Native Americans were the Powhatan. They were made up of many tribes. Chief Powhatan ruled the group.

The Powhatan lived in Virginia's coastal plain. They built homes along the rivers. Their homes were made of **sapling** frames covered with **reed** mats.

The Powhatan traveled the rivers in canoes. They made clothing from deer hides. They hunted, gathered roots and berries, and planted corn and squash.

A Native American village in the Virginia Colony

European Explorers

Giovanni da Verrazzano (gee-oh-VAH-nee dah ver-rah-ZAH-noh) was the first European to discover present-day Virginia. In 1524, he sailed along Virginia's coast.

Around 1559, Spain sent explorers to Virginia. They took a Powhatan boy back to Spain. He became a Christian. In 1570, he returned to Virginia with **missionaries**. They tried to convert other Native Americans. But the mission failed.

Next, England became interested in Virginia. Sir Walter Raleigh sent two ships to explore the land in 1584. The ships' captains told of Virginia's beauty and wealth.

Raleigh sent colonists to Virginia in 1585. They settled on Roanoke Island. But they soon ran out of food. In 1586, Sir Francis Drake visited Roanoke Island. He took the hungry colonists back to England.

Raleigh sent more colonists to Roanoke Island in 1587. The colonists built a settlement. But the next supply ship did not arrive until 1590. By then, the colonists had all disappeared. This is called the Lost Colony of Roanoke.

Sir Walter Raleigh

The Virginia Colony

In 1606, businessmen formed the Virginia Company in England. They gave the name Virginia to all the land from Canada down to Florida. Then they sent 120 colonists to North America. They hoped the colonists would find gold and silver there.

The colonists traveled on ships called the *Discovery*, the *Susan Constant*, and the *Godspeed*. In May 1607, the colonists founded the Virginia Colony. It was England's first permanent colony in North America.

Captain John Smith led the colonists. Some explored the land. Others searched for gold and silver. Some began building a settlement called James Fort.

James Fort was surrounded by a triangle-shaped fence. The corners of the fence had watchtowers. From there, the colonists could defend the fort from attacks.

Inside the fort, colonists built wood houses with thatched roofs. They also built a guardhouse, a church, and a storage house.

More colonists began arriving from England. They built houses outside the fort's wall. The settlement that grew around the fort was called Jamestown.

In 1633, colonists founded another important settlement called Middle Plantation. Later, they renamed it Williamsburg. It was Virginia's capital from 1699 to 1780.

Colonists build Jamestown.

Governing Virginia

Virginia's first governor was Thomas West, Lord De La Warr. England's leader chose the governor. A **council** of upper-class men also ruled Virginia.

In 1619, the House of Burgesses began. It consisted of two colonists elected from each Virginia settlement. They helped govern the colony.

Later that year, Governor George Yeardley held the first Virginia Assembly. It made decisions about the colony. Its members included the governor, the council, and the House of Burgesses. It was North America's first representative government.

Virginia had to follow many of England's laws. In 1651, England passed a new law called the First Navigation Act. It said the colonists could only sell their goods to England. But England paid them little.

The First Navigation Act made the colonists poor. And Native Americans were attacking their settlements. Life in the colony had become difficult. But Governor William Berkeley did little to help the colonists.

The colonists were upset with the government. So in 1676, colonist Nathaniel Bacon led a **rebellion**. He and his followers attacked the Native Americans. And they burned Jamestown. But then Bacon died of a fever. Berkeley returned to power.

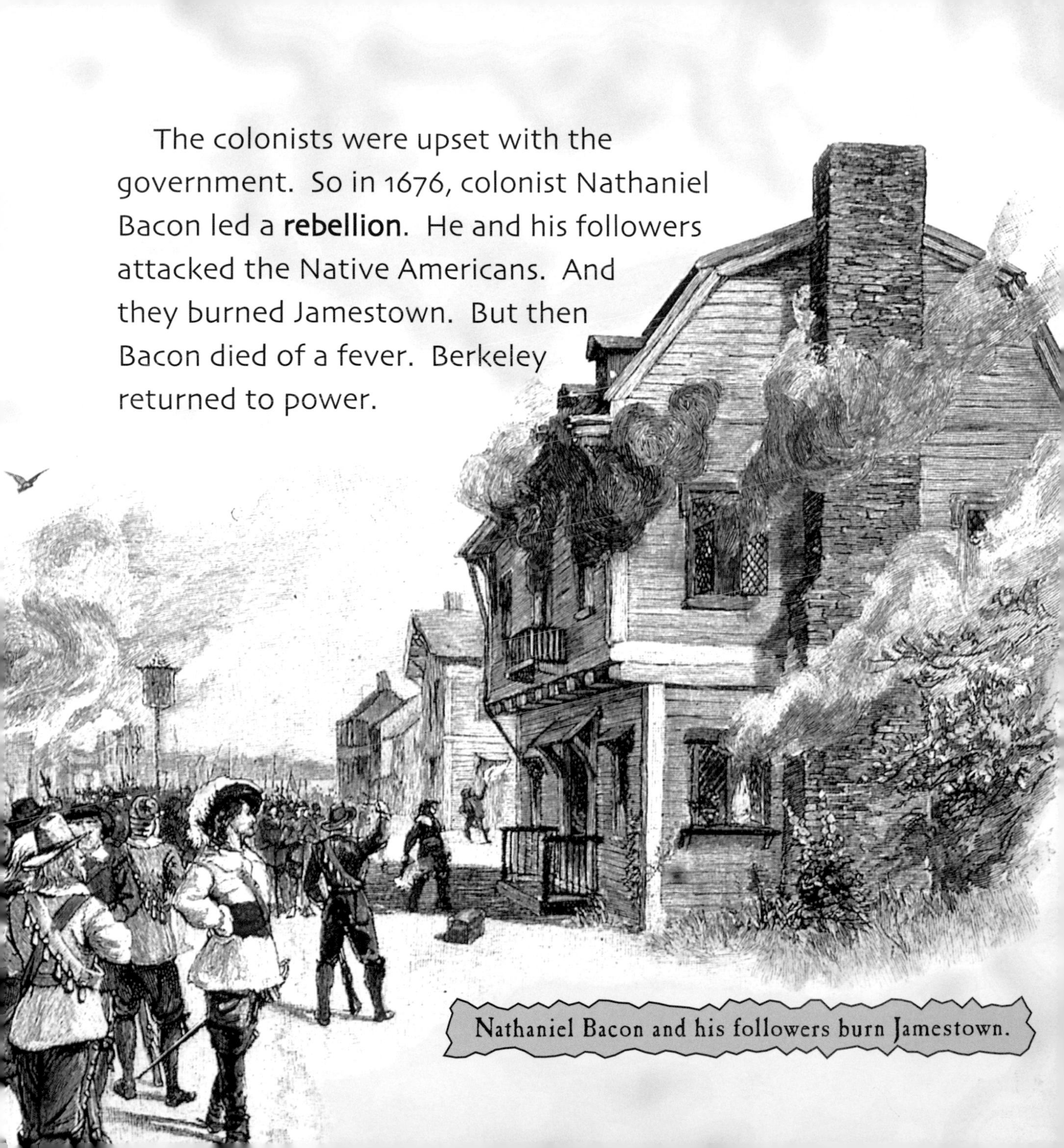

Nathaniel Bacon and his followers burn Jamestown.

Life in the Colony

Virginia's first colonists were all men. They were mostly English gentlemen. The gentlemen came from rich families. Servants had always done work for them. So the gentlemen did not know how to build, plant, or hunt.

The gentlemen soon learned how to work so they could survive. Carpenters, masons, and farmers began to arrive in the colony, too. The men put up buildings, farmed, and ran the government.

At first, few women came to Virginia. The first women in the colony were gentlemens' wives. Later, other women came to the colony to marry the men there. Women kept house, made clothing, and cooked meals.

Virginia's official church was the Church of England. But soon Quakers, Presbyterians (press-buh-TEER-e-unz), Huguenots (HEW-ga-notz), and other religious groups arrived in the colony, too.

Colonists observed religious holidays. They celebrated Christmas, Epiphany (uh-PIFF-ah-nee), Lent, Easter, and Pentecost. On these holidays, colonists prayed and feasted.

Wives for the colonists arrive at Jamestown.

Earning a Living

The colonists found no gold or silver in Virginia. So they looked for other ways to earn money. Virginia's first **export** was lumber. Soon, Virginians began making glass, barrels, boats, and tar.

In 1612, colonist John Rolfe planted Spanish tobacco in Virginia. It grew well. Europeans bought lots of this tobacco from Virginia. This made Virginia's **economy** strong.

Colonists grew tobacco crops along Virginia's rivers and creeks. They packed harvested tobacco leaves into barrels called hogsheads. Workers rolled hogsheads to the James River, loaded them onto ships, and sent them to Europe.

Harvesting tobacco required many workers. In 1619, a Dutch ship arrived with many Africans aboard. The Dutch sold the Africans to the colonists. The Africans worked as slaves on the tobacco farms.

Slave labor allowed tobacco farms to grow and earn money. Slaves supported Virginia's tobacco farms for many years. But some people thought it was wrong to own slaves. In 1865, the Thirteenth **Amendment** made slavery illegal.

Colonists roll hogsheads onto ships bound for England.

Colonial Food

Early colonists had a hard time finding food. Native Americans introduced them to a new food called corn. Soon, colonists were eating boiled corn, roasted corn, and corn bread.

Later, colonists grew their own wheat, corn, and other vegetables. They learned to store food in cellars and **icehouses**. This way, they had plenty to eat during winter.

Colonists had settled close to the sea. So, they ate a lot of seafood. They ate shad, herring, oysters, and clams.

Stew was a popular meal, too. Colonists often prepared a stew called succotash. It was made of corn and butter beans. Colonists also liked Brunswick stew. It was made of squirrel meat and vegetables.

Colonists also enjoyed eating pork. Pigs were easy to bring to Virginia on ships. And the pigs didn't need to be fenced in or fed regularly. In the fall, the pigs were butchered. The meat was **cured** with sugar and smoke.

At first, colonists had little clean water to drink. The bad water made many colonists sick. Some colonists died. So they made their own beer, cider, and brandy.

Colonial women cooked for their families.

Clothing

Rich Virginians wore clothing from England. Men wore white shirts with lace collars. Their coats and pants were made of silk. They wore leather shoes and hats. Women wore dresses made of silk, velvet, satin, or broadcloth.

Common Virginians did not have much money. They could not afford to buy clothes from England. So they made their own clothes from wool and flax.

Farmers grew flax. It is a plant with long, silklike fibers. Women and girls spun the fibers into thread. Then they wove the thread into a cloth called linen. Women then made clothing from this cloth.

Colonists also tanned their own leather. First, they soaked animal hides in **lime** and water. Then they buried the hides in pits filled with tree bark. Finally, they rubbed the hides with grease to make them waterproof. Colonists made shoes, belts, hats, and pouches from leather.

Colonists used spinning wheels to turn flax into thread.

Wealthy colonists wore fancy clothing from England.

The First Homes

Virginians had many choices of building materials. There was plenty of lumber, limestone, and fieldstone. Colonists also made bricks from clay.

Early colonists made their homes using wattle and daub. They drove wooden stakes, called wattles, into the ground. They wove branches and twigs between the stakes. Then they covered the stakes and branches with mud, or daub. The houses had thatched roofs.

Most homes had one room. A family cooked, ate, slept, read, and spun thread all in this one room. The house usually had one large fireplace. It was used both for cooking and heating the house.

Some homes were larger. A successful farmer's home often had several buildings. This separated living and working areas.

Later, colonists built brick row houses. Row houses were popular in England. They are houses attached to each other in a long row. They were often two stories high. They had steep roofs and narrow windows.

As more colonists arrived, they built new styles of homes. For example, colonists from Germany and Scandinavia built log homes.

A reconstruction of Jamestown's wattle and daub houses

Growing up in Virginia

Colonial children worked hard helping their parents. They learned to hunt, cook, and sew. When they had free time, children played games such as tag and hide-and-seek.

Virginians followed the English rule that education was for the rich only. Rich people usually hired **tutors** to teach their children at home. Girls learned to read, write, and do simple math. Boys prepared for college.

Virginia's first free school was established in 1635. There, common students learned from **hornbooks**. They learned the alphabet, numbers, and the Lord's Prayer.

Many young Virginians became **apprentices**. Girl apprentices learned household skills such as cooking, sewing, and weaving. Boy apprentices learned a trade, such as blacksmithing or tailoring.

Virginia's first university was the College of William and Mary. It was established in 1693. Phi Beta Kappa began there in 1776. It is the country's oldest honor society.

The A.B.C
set forthe by the Kynges maiestie and his Clergye, and commaunded to be taught through out all his Realme. All other utterly set a part, as the teachers thereof tender his graces fauour.
In the name of the Father, and of the Sonne, and of the holye Ghoste: So be it.

A hornbook

Native Americans

Many Powhatans lived near the colonists. At first, everyone got along. But soon, colonists wanted to convert the Powhatan to Christianity. And colonists also wanted to settle on Powhatan land.

For years, the colonists and the Powhatan fought. Then in 1614, Chief Powhatan's daughter, Pocahontas, married the colonist John Rolfe. This brought peace. It lasted until Chief Powhatan died in 1618.

Then Opechancanough (oh-pah-CHAN-cah-no) became the new chief. He disliked the colonists. He led an attack against Jamestown in 1622. Of the 1,250 colonists, 350 were killed.

After this, the colonists and Powhatans fought violently. In 1644, the Powhatan attacked the colonists a second time. They killed many colonists. Opechancanough was also captured and killed.

Soon, Virginia's colonists began to move farther west. They met tribes that spoke Sioux and Iroquois languages. These tribes fought the colonists to save their land. But the colonists forced them out.

Chief Opechancanough prepares his men for war against the Virginia colonists.

As Virginia grew, many Native Americans moved farther west. Others died from diseases that the colonists had brought from Europe. Later, some moved to **reservations**.

The Road to Statehood

In 1754, French colonists built forts along the Ohio River. Virginians claimed the land was part of Virginia. This started the **French and Indian War**. It lasted nine years.

To pay for the war, England's **Parliament** charged the colonies taxes. The Stamp Act began in 1765. It charged a tax on paper goods. The tax affected nearly all colonists.

In Virginia, Patrick Henry spoke against the Stamp Act. He and other colonists thought it was unfair. No one represented the colonists in Parliament. This meant no one stood up for the colonists' rights.

Colonists grew tired of England's new taxes. They wanted to govern themselves. This angered the English. So they attacked the colonies in 1775. This attack started the American Revolution.

On July 4, 1776, the colonies adopted the Declaration of Independence. Thomas Jefferson of Virginia had written it. It said the colonies were independent states.

In 1781, the English surrendered at Yorktown, Virginia. Two years later, the colonists officially won the war.

Virginia became the tenth state on June 25, 1788. A year later, George Washington became the first U.S. president.

Over the years, Virginia has continued to grow. Today, its leaders still shape American government. And its historic sites remind visitors how America began.

Virginia's George Washington takes the oath of office as America's first president.

TIMELINE

1524 - Giovanni da Verrazzano is first European to sail past present-day Virginia
1559 - Spaniards explore Virginia
1584 - Sir Walter Raleigh sends two ships to explore Virginia
1585 - Raleigh sends colonists to Roanoke Island
1586 - Roanoke colonists return to England
1587 - Raleigh sends more colonists to Roanoke Island; they disappear
1606 - Virginia Company forms in England, sends colonists to establish Virginia Colony
1607 - Englishmen establish Virginia Colony
1612 - John Rolfe plants first Spanish tobacco
1619 - House of Burgesses meets for first time; Governor Yeardley holds first meeting of Virginia Assembly; first African slaves arrive in Virginia
1622 - Powhatan attack colonists
1633 - Colonists found Middle Plantation (Williamsburg)
1635 - Virginia's first free school established
1644 - Powhatan attack colonists
1651 - First Navigation Act passed
1676 - Nathaniel Bacon leads rebellion
1754 - French and Indian War begins; ends nine years later
1765 - Stamp Act takes effect
1775 - American Revolution begins
1776 - Colonies adopt the Declaration of Independence
1781 - English surrender; war officially ends two years later
1788 - Virginia becomes a state

Glossary

Amendment - a change to the U.S. Constitution.
apprentice - a person who learns a trade from a skilled worker.
council - a group of people who meet, usually to make decisions.
cure - to prepare meat so that it can be eaten several months later.
economy - the way a colony uses its money, goods, and natural resources.
export - goods sent to another country for sale or trade.
French and Indian War - 1754 to 1763. A series of battles fought for control of land in North America. England and its colonies fought against France, its colonies, and several Native American tribes.
hornbook - a sheet of paper used to teach children how to read. The paper was fastened to a frame and handle.
icehouse - a building that stores ice during the summer.
lime - a white substance that comes from limestone, shells, or bone.
missionary - a person who spreads a church's religion.
Parliament - England's lawmaking group.
plateau - a raised area of flat land.
rebellion - an attack against the government.
reed - a kind of tall grass.
reservation - land set aside by the government for Native Americans to live on.
sapling - a thin, young tree.
tutor - a teacher who gives private lessons.

Web Sites

Colonial National Historic Park
http://www.nps.gov/colo/Jthanout/JTBriefs.html
This site is sponsored by the National Park Service. It has several articles on daily life in the Jamestown settlement.

Jamestown Rediscovery
http://www.apva.org/jr.html
This site is sponsored by the Association for the Preservation of Virginia Antiquities. It has a history of Jamestown, pictures of the settlement's remains, and visitor information.

These sites are subject to change. Go to your favorite search engine and type in Virginia Colony for more sites.

Index